John Evelyn Barlas

**Selections from Songs of a Bayadere and Songs of a troubadour**

John Evelyn Barlas

**Selections from Songs of a Bayadere and Songs of a troubadour**

ISBN/EAN: 9783337408602

Printed in Europe, USA, Canada, Australia, Japan

Cover: Foto ©Thomas Meinert / pixelio.de

More available books at **www.hansebooks.com**

SELECTIONS FROM

# Songs of a Bayadere

And

# Songs of a Troubadour.

BY

EVELYN DOUGLAS

DUNDEE:

PRINTED BY JAMES P. MATHEW & CO., 17 COWGATE.

———

1893.

# CONTENTS.

## From Songs of a Bayadere.

## From Songs of a Troubadour.

FROM

# Songs of a Bayadere.

(1890.)

# The Priest of Beauty.

Looms in the perfumed Indian night
  A mystic dome with towers
Of fretted ivory, and marble white,
  And scarlet jewel flowers.

An amorous king, long dead, I ween,
  In that hot and heavy clime,
Built it to bury his fairest queen,
  A marvel to all time.

And the aloes breathe in the orient air
  That tale of love and pride;
And the flowering shrubs send up like prayer
  Sweet incense to his bride.

For she was the loveliest woman born,
  With music in her breath;
And he loved her with love that was half forlorn,
  Because he had heard of death.

And out of the west and out of the east
  The people came to pray,
And he built her a temple and was her priest,
  And served her night and day.

For 'twixt the earth and the stars above
  He was the wisest man;
And beauty he loved with a madman's love,
  As only madmen can.

So all her life he built her a tomb
  Of marbles costly and rare,
Full of odour, and sumptuous gloom,
  And colour, and love's despair;

With amber silks and jewels of light;
  With fountains and courts and bowers;
With alabaster pillars as white
  And waxen as lotus-flowers.


For she was the loveliest woman born,
  And he was the noblest sage;
And he loved her with love that was partly scorn,
  Because he had seen old age.


For he said, " If I tarry for Death's own time
  Her beauty will melt like foam;
'Twere best she should die in her beauty's prime
  And sleep in her beautiful home."


So he slew her, and laid her in costly spice
  And frankincense and myrrh,
And wrapped her in raiment of fabulous price,
  And shed no tear for her.

# The Priestess of Athor.

WHERE Egypt's holy river
　Flows through the haunted nights,
Stood once the city of Memphis,
　Full of lutes and lights.

And there the child of Athor—
　A priestess pure and fair,
Lost in the temple garden,
　In the aloe-scented air—

Found love in the moonlit roses,
　Whose perfume told her this—
That the gods would all leave heaven
　For one warm human kiss;

12

Found love in the wandering breezes,
    Whose music told her this—
That the gods are dying in heaven
    For the want of a human kiss ;

Found love in the hallowed waters,
    And love in the stars above ;
And learnt that the gods are lonely,
    And jealous of human love.

# The Lily and Lotus.

THERE grew a flower in Babylon
    Whose perfume makes young lovers weep;
On it Assyrian moonlight shone;
    Euphrates murmured it to sleep.
It brings back old forgotten dreams;
    Its petals breathe a dead love's kiss;
Astarte bathed it in her beams
    In the gardens of Semiramis.

But Egypt has a sweeter bloom—
    The lotus of forgetful breath :
Swathed and embalmed in spicèd gloom,
    The sad Nile sobbed its dreams to death.
It soothes remembered loves to rest
    As quiet as death's waxen lid;
They laid it on Nitocris' breast
    Beneath her silent pyramid.

# The Ruins of Nineveh.

WHERE Nineveh in ruin sleeps,
  Two ruined lives lie low,
Whose hearts leapt as your heart now leaps
  Thousands of years ago.

They loved, they struggled but to fail,
  And then they sank and died;
How shall I tell you all the tale
  So many ages hide?

I know her heart in silence broke,
  His pain was cruel and slow,
And then they slept and never woke,
  And that is all I know.

15

I guess the world then, as to-day,
  Scorned love and loveliness,
And that the world stood in their way,
  And that is all I guess.

I feel they must have moved apart,
  And both kept under seal
Of smiling face a broken heart,
  And that is all I feel.

I fear that they were slowly crushed,
  And prayed, and none would hear,
And then their beating hearts were hushed,
  And that was all, I fear.

Perhaps the desert wind that blows
  O'er ruined Nineveh
More of that old-world story knows,
  And if it cared, could say.

Still to eternity time creeps;
  And there still crumbling slow
The ruined centuries lie in heaps,
  Two ruined hearts below.


I hope their secret was well kept,
  As that of me and you,
And slept safe with them when they slept,
  And that they both died true.


I trust their troth was truly kept,
  As we have kept our trust,
And that there was some friend who wept
  Upon their bitter dust.


I pray they had some hours of joy,
  As you and I to-day,
Some hope the world could not destroy—
  And that is all I pray.

But, gentle lady, do not weep;
  It does not matter now.
Beneath the ruined walls they sleep
  With placid lips and brow.

Two heaps of dust there side by side,
  What can they feel or know?
These lovers suffered, failed, and died
  Thousands of years ago.

# In Egyptian Thebes.

You are not strange to me, I know;
Somewhere I saw you long ago,
When I was not so forlorn,
In a dream ere I was born.

'Twas in a garden by the Nile,
Where the aloe-flowers did smile;
And basking by the yellow deep,
Thebes lay with giant walls asleep.

I know you gave me once a kiss;
'Twas underneath a precipice,
Monstrous marble masonry
Towering black into the sky,

Walls on walls, a dizzy pile,
O'er a garden by the Nile,
Where Thebes lay by the sacred stream,
Wrapped in her hundred gates, to dream.

# The Mummy's Love Story.

Where in a stone sarcophagus
  Lay in embalmed repose
A shape with robes luxurious,
  They found a faded rose.

Perhaps it was an amorous boy
  That to a princess gave
Some token of their secret joy,
  That she wore to the grave.

Perhaps it was a murdered youth
  Sent on the eve of doom
An emblem of forgiving truth,
  His queen wore to the tomb.

Who knows? But there it speaks for her
  Of sorrows long past now,
When neither joy nor pain can stir
  The arch of her calm brow.


And so, when you have let me die,
  And you too are at rest,
Some trinket of my gift may lie
  On your repentant breast.


And when our language is forgot,
  Some lover of old scenes
May find it in a haunted spot,
  And wonder what it means.

# Death.

A GREEK girl came to Pharaoh's bed,
  Who died upon her bridal night.
At morn he saw her lying dead,
  And deemed she lived, she was so white.

And when on snowy linen strown
  She lay embalmed as if she dreamed,
He could not feel himself alone,
  So beautiful the body seemed.

He sat and stroked her golden hair,
  And looked and looked in her dead eyes;
He said, "She is forever fair;
  How like a statue there she lies!"

He kissed her lips though they were cold,
　And never missed the mortal breath;
He said, "She never will be old,
　Or die, for she has done with death."

Till fire into his palace crept,
　And burned his dead, his lovely bride.
Then Pharaoh rent his robes, and wept,
　And fell upon his sword, and died.

FROM

# Songs of a Troubadour.

(1890.)

# The Priest of Love.

In Sicily in the days of art
  A painter prince held sway,
Who loved one lady with all his heart
  And dreamed of her night and day.

She was a girl of scarce thirteen,
  And he was but a youth ;
Yet he sware none other should be his queen,
  And kept his oath with truth.

And still as she grew he built her a home,
  That the years less long might seem,
Out on an island, girt with the foam,
  Beautiful as a dream.

And he called the masters from every part,
  Of temper, and tint, and tone,
Who moulded in metal miraculous art,
  Or wrought it in colour or stone,

All carvers of wood and silver and gold,
  All weavers that loved the loom,
To make her a palace of perfect mould,
  And fill it with tender bloom.

And he sent for marbles out of the isles,
  Rose-red and white as snow,
And made a dome that shone for miles
  In the ruddy evening glow.

And the palace grew, and the maiden grew
  In stature and beauty and grace
Year by year—for shape and for hue,
  A wonderful woman's face.

And ever of marbles from far-off isles,
    Like music soft and slow,
Rose fluted pillars and fretted piles,
    And hung in the wave below,

With many a cupola poised above,
    And many a sculptured frieze,
That filled with anguish of hopeless love
    The amorous ocean breeze.

And he hung rich arras about the place,
    Wrought in a distant clime,
With love, and passion, and war, and the chase,
    And gods of the olden time;

And he steeped his brush in the hues of love,
    His soul in the poet's themes,
And filled the walls and the ceilings above
    With forms as fair as dreams;

And he melted his heart to heavenly hues,
  And bathed the grainèd glass
In burning reds and beautiful blues,
  And greens as soft as grass;

And he fetched rare marbles from far-off isles
  For the sculptors, as white as snow,
Who made them smile immortal smiles,
  With love immortal glow.

And the palace grew and the maiden grew
  In beauty side by side;
And when both were perfect in form and hue,
  And ready—the maiden died.

Then he shut himself up in the palace alone,
  With the statues and his despair,
And his young dead bride as cold as stone,
  And fired it, and perished there.

And the red flame shone to the far-off isles
  Over the ocean-flow,
And the sky was red for miles and miles,
  And the sea lay red below.

# The Broken Lute.

THERE was a gallant troubadour
  Who loved his lady and his lute;
But she was false, and then he tore
  The strings, and struck his darling mute.

It nevermore shall sound her praise;
  Far from his breast it sleeps apart:
And when they ask, the poet says—
  "I broke it when she broke my heart."

# The Troubadour Monk.

WHEN the thin bell to vespers calls,
  And shines the evening star,
He looks out from the convent walls
  Across the window-bar;
He hears the organ's muttered growl
  Through the open chapel door—
The gloomy monk in the ebon cowl,
  That was a troubadour.

Then will he take down with a sigh
  The lute that oft hath played
A prelude 'neath a balcony
  Unto a serenade;
A moment on the mute strings brood,
  And pass his fingers o'er—
The phantom in the night-black hood,
  That was a troubadour.

33

"Ah shadows from the cloister flung,
  To song and love denied!
Hard narrow hearts to live among,
  With the great warm world outside!
Ah tuneless throats, dull eyes that scowl!
  Ah hymns of saintly lore,
That I must mutter in my cowl,
  Who was a troubadour!


"The moon shines fair, the sky is bright;
  On such a night as this,
When all the windows were alight,
  I saw young lovers kiss;
White hands, where latticed panes lay ope,
  Drew curtains by the score,
To hear this dumb thing in a cope,
  That was a troubadour.

34

"The moon shines fair, the deep skies dream;
  On such a night as this
I heard steel clash and women scream
  And jealous curses hiss;
I heard the nightingale, the owl,
  Heard love, and hate, and more—
All life's loud tide, till death's dumb cowl
  Stifled the troubadour.


"Ah to sing now the songs I sung,
  To walk the warm world wide,
The lute across my shoulder slung,
  A sharp sword at my side!
The zither-string, the rapier-stroke!
  To sing, to love once more—
Love? No; forever 'neath the cloak
  Must hide the troubadour.

"False hope of peace to which I clung,
   Love left, song laid aside!
Poor darkened mind, poor lute unstrung,
   And thou, my poor false bride!
Mad monks that chant, mad dogs that howl,
   Mad moonlight on the floor!
Mad grinning death's-head in a cowl,
   That was a troubadour."

# The Serenade.

## I.

O lady, in your dim sweet dreams,
Like far-off woods my singing seems,
Like woods, and winds, and far-off streams,
Sea-murmurs mingled with moonbeams.

O lady mine, the cold stars shine;
My heart is heavy; I cannot weep.
For mercy's sake, for love's, awake!
Or else forever I must sleep.

O lady love, in slumber laid,
Listen to my serenade.

## II.

You cannot hear what my lute saith,
But I can hear your soft, calm breath.
Sweet sleep is yours that lingereth,
But I must sleep in lasting death.

    O lady mine, the chill stars shine,
      My heart is heavy, and I must weep;
    For mercy's sake, for love's, awake!
      I fain would kiss thee ere I sleep.

O lady love, in slumber laid,
Listen to my serenade.

# The Gift.

WHAT shall I send my lady fair
  To mind her of my love?
A ribbon-string, a lock of hair,
  A garter, fan, or glove?

A falcon, keen-eyed as the day,
  To sit upon her wrist,
And flap his wings and fly away
  When she may cry, "Hist! hist!"

A Spanish steed as white as milk,
  True to her least command,
All in a net of golden silk,
  To feed out of her hand?

A strong sleuth-hound of kingly breed
  To come unto her call,
Deep-jowled, of matchless strength and speed,
  To see her safe through all?

A soft, a tender cooing dove
  To nestle in her breast,
And mind her of my absent love
  When she is in her nest?

A lute of deep and tender tone
  Her fingers fair can play,
That she may not be quite alone
  When I am far away?

A mirror fair of silver sheen
  Encased in mother-o'-pearl,
To let her beauty well be seen
  When she would set a curl?

A missal with a clasp of gold
  And plates like coloured glass,
For her dainty little hand to hold
  When she would go to mass?

A silken veil of silver hue
  Which she can drop or lift,
To hide her blushing face from view
  When she would go to shrift?

A string of amber beads to count
  Her pretty sins, ywis,
And reckon up the long amount
  Of her infidelities?

A coil of pearls to clasp her neck,
  That mocks their dusky hues,
To hide each little purple speck
  Where a kiss has left a bruise?

A fan, when lovers round her swarm,
  O'er which to dart her glance,
Or to hide her blushing cheek when warm
  In the pauses of the dance ?

A cushion, where at feet of her
  Some lute-player may kneel ?
A pen to write a love letter ?
  A Cupid on a seal ?

A withered rose that should be fair,
  Heart-cankered in the bud ?—
Ah, no, a tress of my dead hair
  Dabbled in my heart's blood.

# The Death of Garth.

KING Sigmund sailed forth in the foam
  Unto a far-off strand,
And brought a strange king's daughter home,
  A wonder to the land.

"Now, call ye Garth, my minstrel fair,
  To play before my queen;
For well I wot, though white his hair,
  Such eyes he hath not seen."

White was the poet's hair; the shade
  Deep on his brows had grown;
And many a love-song he had made,
  But love he had not known.

For he had sung and he had fought
  Until his hair was white;
But never seen the eyes he sought,
  Save in the dreams of night.

The harp was brought, the bard obeyed,
  And bowed before the throne;
And many a love-song he had made,
  But love he had not known.

But when he raised his voice to sing,
  His eyes to hers, with pain
His hand was numbed upon the string,
  The song within his brain.

Then cried the king: "Is song divine?
  Can age prevail o'er art?
Go, fetch a bowl of royal wine
  To cheer the poet's heart."

"It is not age," the poet said,
  "Not age," he cried,—"despair!
For I shall soon be with the dead,
  And, ah! she is too fair."

They brought the wine; the minstrel quaffed,
  But ere he lipped the bowl,
He cast a poison in the draught
  That freed his tortured soul.

And now he treads the deathless plain
  And drinks the deathless air,
Chanting his lonely last refrain—
  "For, ah! she is too fair."

# The Lady's Secret.

THERE lived a lady long ago,
  Whose beauty dazzled many lands;
Her bosom was as white as snow,
  But whiter were her lovely hands.

Not till her death it reached men's ears
  Why those white hands made all hearts ache.
She washed them in love's hopeless tears
  And blood of men slain for her sake.

# The Little Page.

Up in the morning rose the queen,
   And the morning of her age,
And forth into the forest green
   Rode with her little page.

He was a lonely orphan boy,
   Son of a gentle sire,
And she had taken pride and joy
   To rear him for her squire.

And often in his childish way—
   He was not yet fourteen—
"How can I thank you?" he would say,
   "So kind to me you 've been."

And he was generous and brave
    And true as tempered steel;
He loved to sing her a gentle stave,
    And at her feet to kneel.

Up in the morning rose the queen,
    And took her little page,
A gentle child of scarce fourteen,
    From noble parentage.

And forth she fared with merry cheer
    To ply the royal art;
And aiming at a fallow deer
    She pierced the poor boy's heart.

Then from the ground with smile so sweet
    He struggled to her side,
And lay down bleeding at her feet,
    And kissed her hand, and died.

And dying, in his childish way—
He was not yet fourteen—
"How shall I thank you?" he did say,
"So kind to me you've been.

"And many a kind act you have done,
And loyal I have been;
But this of all the kindest one,
The best for me, my queen."

# Lute and Sword.

## A Song of Chatelar.

No knight, no lord
  With titles varnished,
My lute, my sword
  I keep untarnished.
Poet and soldier, thy fair hand
I kiss, and wait for thy command.

My humble suit
  Can ne'er deserve thee;
My sword, my lute
  May haply serve thee.
Lady, I lay them at thy feet;
Dispose of them as is but meet.

Lady, a word,
  A lifted finger!
Hand, lute, sword
  Shall never linger.
Lady, I am not mine, but thine;
My spirit kneels at thy pure shrine.

  Trembling and mute,
    Thy name unnamèd;
  With sword and lute,
    Abashed, ashamèd
I wait. Nor think nor plead can I;
Speak for me; bid me live or die.

  Beloved, adored,
    I dare not woo thee.
  Life, lute, soul, sword
    I offer to thee.
Lady, I lay them at thy feet,
Dispose of them as is but meet.

(1888.)

# The Last Serenade.

THE moonlight sleeps upon the lake,
   And music on my heart.
O lady mine, awake, awake,
   For love is where thou art.
The ripple sobs below the boat,
The swan sleeps on the castle moat,
The water-lilies round me float,
   And yet we are apart.

The stars are out, the love-bird calls,
   Men sleep, the hour is late;
The shadow of the castle falls
   Across my heart like fate.
The wind awakes among the woods,
And murmurs from the solitudes,
The heart-sick owl i' the ivy broods,
   And I am here and wait.

(1888.)

# The Ballad of the Loyal Traitor.

In Britain dwelt an ancient king
  Who had a lovely wife  ·
And one fair squire who wore his ring
  And loved him as his life.

Now, so it happed, a treason loath
  To that his squire fell known,
Of twenty knights who sware an oath
  To slay him on his throne.

And when to hall those traitors came
  To do their evil part,
The squire came twixt the king and them
  Who stabbed him to the heart.

The king bowed low his hoary head,
  And tore his beard so white;
"Ah, would," he cried, "that I were dead,
  Not thou, my brave boy-knight!"

The queen sat pale upon her throne;
  "And he so young!" she cried,
"And woman's love he hath not known,
  And now death is his bride."

The young maids combed his rich black hair,
  And wept for very love.
The good leech laid the heart-wound bare
  And found—the young queen's glove.

Then to his feet the king did start,
  His silver beard gan rend:
"Would that the knife had pierced my heart,
  Not the treachery of my friend!"

Then fell the king upon his face,
    Hid in his purple weeds :
"Better the wound that kills disgrace
    Than love that lives and bleeds."

# The Black Troubadour.

'NEATH trellised window and porch in bloom,
  White roses clamber o'er,
In jetty mantle and sable plume
  Carols the troubadour.

He sings to her of love and art,
  The joy to sin and roam;
He steals away her virgin heart
  From her father's quiet home.

'Neath trellised window and porch in bloom,
  Red roses ramble o'er,
In sable feather and cloak of gloom
  Stands Sin, the troubadour.

He wheedles her with honeyed lies,
  Till at heaven's last low verge
The sun sets blushing, the stars arise ;
  And then he chants a dirge.

Under the window and porch in bloom
  Life's roses riot o'er,
In black hearse-feather and pall from the tomb
Sings Death, the troubadour.

www.ingramcontent.com/pod-product-compliance
Lightning Source LLC
Chambersburg PA
CBHW030721110426
42739CB00030B/1131